KANSAS STATE CAPITOL

FACTS

The total cost of original construction (1866 to 1903) on the Kansas State Capitol was $3,200,588.92. The building's footprint is 57,600 square feet; 399 feet from the north to the south wing, and 386 feet from the east to the west wing. It stands 306 feet from the ground to the top of *Ad Astra's* bow, which is 17 feet higher than the U. S. Capitol.

This book is dedicated to the people of Kansas, and governors and legislators past and present who saw a vision for the Great State of Kansas.

This book was researched, written, and designed by the staff of the Kansas Historical Society with special credit to Bobbie Athon, Linda Kunkle Park, and Lisa Hecker whose efforts should be acknowledged, along with many other staff. The Historical Society thanks Barry Greis, statehouse architect, Treanor Architects, and JE Dunn Construction for their cooperation. Unless noted all photographs are from the collections of the Kansas Historical Society.

Produced by the Kansas Historical Society for the Kansas Historical Foundation.

©2013
Kansas Historical Foundation
Topeka, Kansas

ABRAHAM LINCOLN

Kansas State Capitol

CONTENTS

Introduction v

Path to Statehood 4

Construction 14

House of Government 44

Artwork 82

Capitol Square 96

Restoration 108

Neighborhood 128

Legacy 146

The Capitol rotunda from third floor looking southeast.
©2013 Architectural Fotographics/Treanor Architects

TOP TO BOTTOM: Stylized ionic capital at top of pilaster on the third floor south wing; balustrade on the first floor staircase west wing; marble in the second floor staircase south wing.

Kansas State Capitol
INTRODUCTION

The Kansas State Capitol is considered the state's greatest architectural treasure. The founders undertook what many thought an impossible task—to create a grand classical structure on the frontier that would symbolize their pride in Kansas' tumultuous path to statehood and their grand hopes for its future. The undertaking was immense and impressive.

Called the Kansas Statehouse as the seat of state government for much of its history, the majestic structure represents Kansas' fascinating past. The long trek to statehood had spanned exploration, removal of native peoples from the East to live alongside native peoples of the plains, and the fight to determine whether Kansas would be free. The state was only five years old when construction began; the Civil War had just ended.

Using materials from the bedrock of Kansas limestone to premier marble from Europe, the Capitol was a labor of love for the early settlers. They envisioned a lasting monument that would incorporate the unique story of the state's history. This building was the investment they made to secure Kansas' place as a leader for the nation.

Under construction for more than 37 years from 1866 to 1903, the statehouse was the place for the daily business of state government. Important, ground-breaking events in state and national history also unfolded within these walls and on these grounds. These stories are told through photographs, documents, and objects from the Capitol's past.

Architectural details embellish the north wing.

Entrance to the Senate Chamber. ©2013 Architectural Fotographics/Treanor Architects

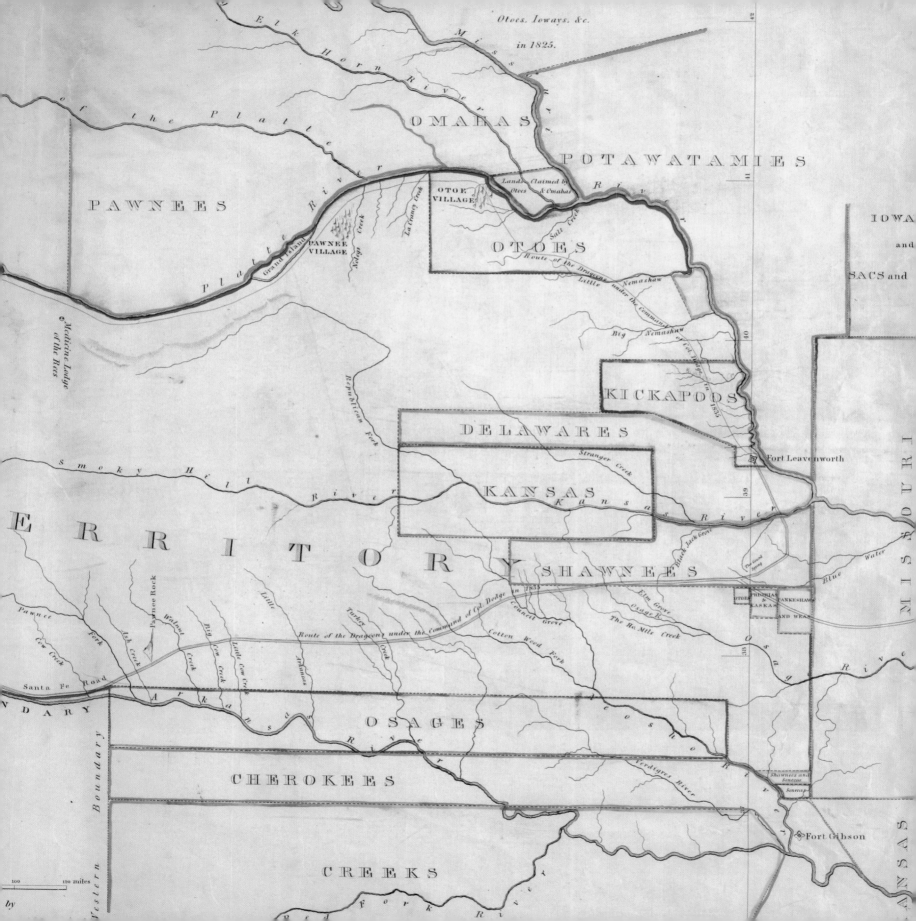

Otoes. Ioways. &c.
in 1825.

Elk Horn River

of the Platte River

Missouri

OMAHAS

POTAWATAMIES

PAWNEES

Platte River
Grand Island
PAWNEE VILLAGE
Nodign Creek
La Fancy Creek
OTOE VILLAGE
Lands Claimed by Otoes & Omahas

IOWAY
and
SACS and

OTOES
Salt Creek
Route of the Dragoons
Little Nemashaw

Medicine Lodge of the Rees

Republican Fork

Big Nemashaw

KICKAPOOS

Smoky Hill River

DELAWARES
Stranger Creek
Fort Leavenworth

KANSAS
Kansas River

E R R I T O R Y

SHAWNEES
Black Jack Grove
The Good Spring
Water
Blue
OTOES PIQUAS & KASKAS
PANKESHAW AND WEA

Route of the Dragoons under the Command of Col. Dodge in 1835
Council Grove
Elm Grove
Osage R.
The Ho Mile Creek

Pawnee Rock
Walnut Creek
Little Cow Creek
Big Cow Creek
Ash Creek
Turkey Creek
Cotton Wood Fork
Arkansas

Pawnee Fork
Cow Creek

Santa Fe Road

Neosho River

B O U N D A R Y
Western Boundary

Arkansas River

O S A G E S

Verdigres River
Shawnees and Senecas
Senecas

CHEROKEES

Fort Gibson

CREEKS

Red Fork River

100   120 miles

by

Kansas State Capitol
PATH TO STATEHOOD

Kansas' trek toward statehood grew out of the nation's emerging thirst for land. Explorers from Europe and the young United States were drawn to the beauty of the prairies.

This was the place where thousands of native peoples from the East and Great Lakes were moved to provide space for new American immigrants. The Indian Removal Act of 1830 resulted in numerous tribes of people coming to Kansas, people with very different cultural traditions. This land was already home to thousands of native plains peoples.

When the eastern United States became populated and immigrants yearned for new lands to settle, they looked west. Both indigenous native peoples and those newly moved to Kansas were occupying prime space for new settlement.

As America became increasingly divided over slavery, states fairly evenly split north and south. The Kansas-Nebraska Act of 1854 allowed voters to determine the fate of the new states. Lawmakers believed that Nebraska would become free while Kansas would be a slave state, maintaining the balance of power. Advocates for and against slavery converged on the new territory leading to the period known as Bleeding Kansas. They would decide Kansas' fate.

OPPOSITE: This 1835 map shows Indian lands stretching across the central plains.

ABOVE: Admit Me Free flag showed support for a free Kansas.

LEFT: Kansas Territory was officially established in 1854 with the passage of the Kansas-Nebraska Act.

PATH TO STATEHOOD TIMELINE

The Osage were among the many tribes in the area.

Westward, Ho by David H. Overmyer

U. S. Congress passes Missouri Compromise, which prohibits slavery in area that will become Kansas Territory

Relocation of Indian tribes from the East to plains begins

Oregon-California Trail opens, hundreds of immigrants cross northeast Kansas headed west

1820　　　**1825**　　　**1843**

1804　　　**1821**　　　**1830**　　　**1850**

Lewis and Clark expedition reaches the confluence of the Missouri and Kansas rivers, documenting the area in their journals

Mexico wins independence from Spain; Santa Fe Trail trade route opens and passes through the area that will be Kansas

U. S. Congress passes the Indian Removal Act trading lands in the East for reservation lands in the West

Compromise of 1850 allows California to enter Union as a free state

Fugitive Slave Act prohibits people from aiding escapees

Lewis and Clark in Kansas by David H. Overmyer

"The Marais des Cygnes Massacre, Kansas," *Beyond the Mississippi,* by Albert D. Richardson

Kansas-Nebraska Act creates two territories and allows settlers to determine whether slavery will be allowed

1854

First territorial legislature meets in Pawnee near Fort Riley

Topeka Constitutional Convention passes first of four constitutions

1855

Bleeding Kansas act of violence – Sack of Lawrence

1856

Lecompton Constitutional Convention passes second of four constitutions

1857

Bleeding Kansas act of violence – Marais des Cygnes Massacre

Leavenworth Constitutional Convention passes third of four constitutions

1858

Wyandotte Constitutional Convention passes fourth and final constitution

1859

U. S. Congress ratifies the Wyandotte Constitution making Kansas a free state

1861

President James Buchanan signs the bill creating the 34th state in the Union

Civil War begins

The Sacking of Lawrence by Lumen Martin Winter

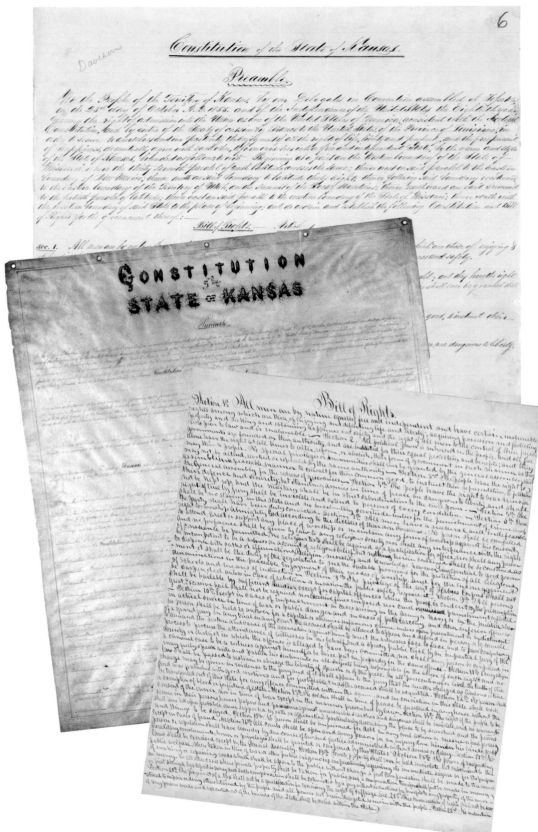

TOP TO BOTTOM: The Topeka Constitution, drafted in 1855, supported the freestaters. The U. S. Congress took no action on this constitution. Courtesy National Archives

The Lecompton Constitution, drafted in 1857, was the second constitution for Kansas Territory. It protected the rights of slave holders. Voters at first approved, then rejected the constitution, which was then rejected by the U. S. Congress.

The Leavenworth Constitution, created in 1858, was the third of the four documents. It banned slavery, provided rights for all male voters, making no distinction between whites and African Americans in terms of civil rights, and provided some protection for women's rights. At the time of its creation, the separate pages were pasted together and rolled into one long scroll. The U. S. Congress did not vote on this constitution.

OPPOSITE: The Wyandotte Constitution, written in 1859, was the fourth and final document. While it prohibited slavery, only white residents obtained full civil rights. Women were allowed to participate in school district elections, to own property, and share equal custody rights of their children. The U. S. Congress approved this document, which became the state constitution.

Kansas State Capitol
CONSTITUTIONS

Most delegates to the first session of Kansas' territorial legislature had been elected by proslavery supporters who crossed the border to vote illegally. The "bogus" legislature convened for four days in summer 1855 in Pawnee, near Fort Riley. The territorial governor repealed most of the laws it passed.

In opposition to the bogus legislature, the free-state Topeka Constitutional Convention met in fall 1855. This first constitution would have prohibited slavery in the new state. Only white males and "civilized" male American Indians could vote.

Proslavery delegates met in fall 1857 in Lecompton. Their constitution allowed voters to choose for or against slavery. Freestaters refused to participate because a vote against slavery allowed Kansans to keep the slaves they already owned. Proslavery voters passed the constitution, which led to months of controversy and a bitter national debate. Kansans voted again a few months later to overwhelmingly defeat the Lecompton Constitution; however, President James Buchanan encouraged the U. S. Congress to ratify the document.

While congressional debate continued, delegates met in spring 1858 in Leavenworth to draft a third constitution. The bill of rights it contained referred to "all men." It prohibited slavery from the state, and eliminated any reference to "white" voters. Kansas voters approved the constitution, but it was abandoned after Congress rejected the Lecompton Constitution later that summer.

In summer 1859 delegates gathered in Wyandotte (near present Kansas City) for the fourth and final constitutional convention. The decision to make Kansas a free state at this point was no surprise. Suffrage was granted only to white men 21 years and older. Women were allowed to participate in school district elections,

to own property, and share equal custody rights of their children, groundbreaking gains for the time. Delegates redefined the western border, which had extended as far as the Continental Divide. Voters approved the document in fall 1859 by a two to one margin.

The free-state Wyandotte Constitution faced heavy opposition from Southern congressmen, yet the House of Representatives approved the document in early 1860. After Abraham Lincoln's election, Southern states began to secede. The day the last of the Southern senators had left, the Senate passed the Kansas bill. The House passed the bill as amended the following week. President James Buchanan, despised by most free-state settlers, signed the bill making Kansas the 34th state on January 29, 1861.

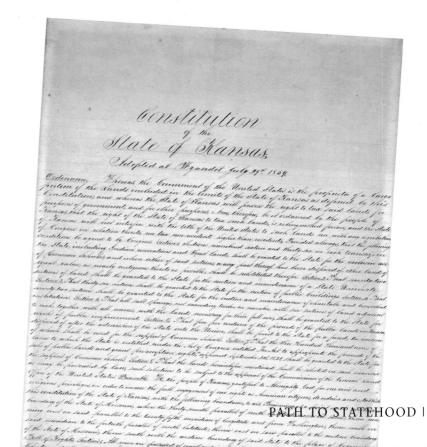

Kansas State Capitol
TOPEKA, CAPITAL CITY

Years before Kansas was opened for settlement, brothers Joseph and Ahcan Pappan established a ferry at the Kansas River crossing near what would become Topeka. Travelers headed west on the Oregon-California Trail and the military trails used this crossing.

When Kansas Territory was opened for settlement in 1854, people from the East settled areas along the waterway. Topeka was one of a number of cities founded during that first year. Several communities began a rigorous competition to be named the capital city.

The contest continued as delegates met in Wyandotte in 1859. There they decided to include a provision that named Topeka as the temporary state capital. On January 29, 1861, when President Buchanan signed the bill making Kansas a state, the Kansas territorial legislature was in session in Lawrence. Governor Charles Robinson took the oath of office as the first governor and ordered the state legislature to convene several weeks later in Topeka.

The legislature had few suitable locations to meet in Topeka. Buildings along Kansas Avenue were used prior to the construction of the Capitol and included Constitution Hall, where the Topeka Constitutional Convention had been held in 1855, located near 5th on Kansas Avenue; the Gale block, between 6th and 7th on Kansas Avenue; and the third floor of the Ritchie block, at 6th and Kansas avenues.

Finally in November 1861 voters made the final selection for Kansas' capital city. With 14,981 votes cast, the top three were: Topeka 7,589; Lawrence 5,194; and Leavenworth 815.

OPPOSITE: This view of Kansas Avenue looks west toward the Capitol, 1871.

TOP: The Topeka Constitutional Convention met in Constitution Hall near 5th on Kansas Avenue in 1855.

ABOVE: This stereograph from Alexander Gardner's series, *Across the Continent on the Union Pacific Railway, Eastern Division, 1867*, looks northeast. In the foreground are construction stones used in building the Capitol; Kansas Avenue can be seen in the background.

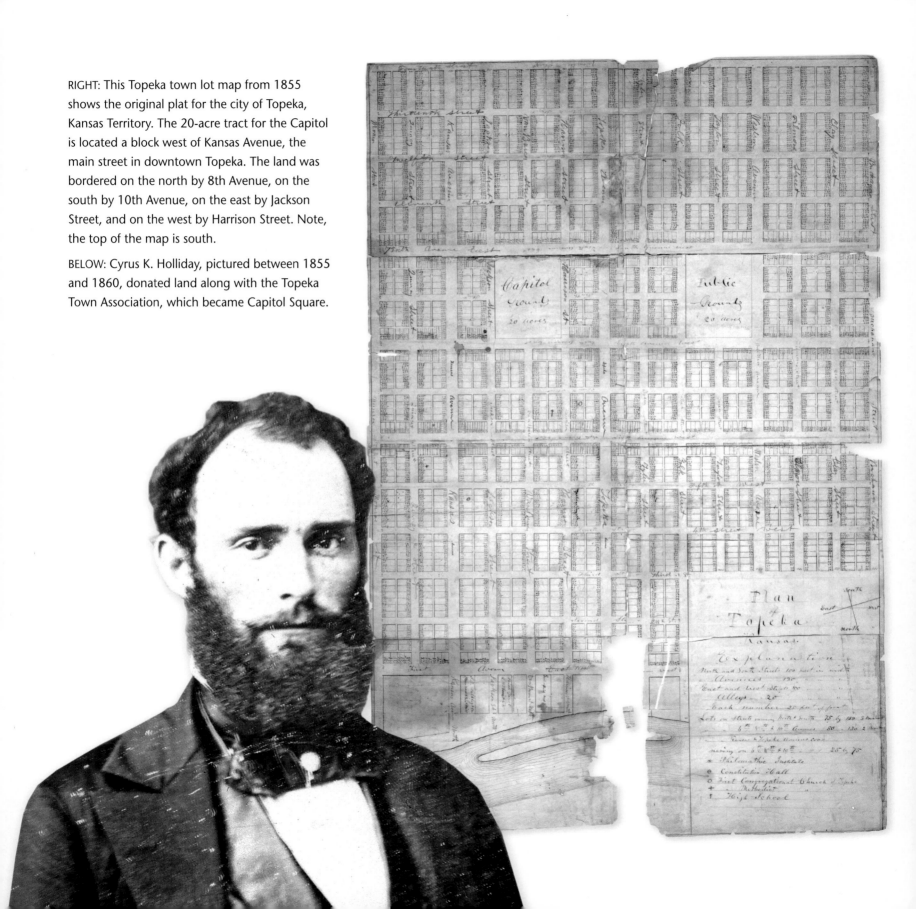

RIGHT: This Topeka town lot map from 1855 shows the original plat for the city of Topeka, Kansas Territory. The 20-acre tract for the Capitol is located a block west of Kansas Avenue, the main street in downtown Topeka. The land was bordered on the north by 8th Avenue, on the south by 10th Avenue, on the east by Jackson Street, and on the west by Harrison Street. Note, the top of the map is south.

BELOW: Cyrus K. Holliday, pictured between 1855 and 1860, donated land along with the Topeka Town Association, which became Capitol Square.

Kansas State Capitol
CYRUS K. HOLLIDAY

Cyrus K. Holliday was among the early settlers who moved west in 1854 to take advantage of new opportunities in Kansas Territory. Originally from Pennsylvania, Holliday became involved in the Free State movement in the new territory.

In November 1854 Holliday wrote to his wife about the city that would become Topeka. "God might have made a better country than the [sic] Kansas but so far as my knowledge extends he certainly never did," Holliday wrote. "I am bound to make it my home if I can at all succeed in making suitable business arrangements. The site of this new city I think is most beautiful—and I know you would be delighted with it."

Nine men, including Holliday, gathered at a log cabin on Kansas Avenue in December 1854, to form the Topeka Town Association. "We are just about in the central portion of the settled territory and with perhaps the best landing and the most eligible site for a city in the entire country," he later wrote to his wife. "A more lovely country, I certainly never saw."

Holliday was elected the first mayor of Topeka. In 1859 Holliday founded the Atchison, Topeka & Santa Fe Railway. Then in 1862 he and the Topeka Town Association donated the 20-acre tract of land to be used for the state capitol.

TOP: Cyrus K. Holliday, front row left, is pictured circa 1861. Holliday, on behalf of the Topeka Town Association, donated 20 acres for the Kansas State Capitol.

ABOVE: Cyrus K. Holliday's diary, written in 1854, describes the settlement that will become Topeka.

The Stone is yellow limestone, and under the skillful manipulation of the workmen, presents a beautiful appearance. It rests in the northeast corner of the building. . .

—*Topeka Weekly Leader*, October 18, 1866

OPPOSITE: This Gardner stereograph shows construction of the east wing with a portion of the completed first floor.

ABOVE: A Gardner photograph taken from the Capitol grounds shows Lincoln College (now Washburn University) at the northeast corner of 10th and Jackson along with other buildings and dwellings.

Kansas State Capitol
CONSTRUCTION

Created as a grand monument to the founders of the free state, the Capitol was meant to be the center of state government. The members of the building committee agreed that Greek and Roman architecture should influence the design; they did not all agree with specific aspects. Multiple designs were reviewed and discussed during the years of construction.

The builders carefully considered the materials that would be used in the construction. They wanted to ensure access to sufficient quantities and maintain high quality. They needed to be able to transport the materials to the work site. In 1866 state geologist Benjamin Franklin Mudge assisted in identifying a limestone bed near Manhattan in Riley County as appropriate, but with no railroads there at the time, it was not possible to ship the stone to Topeka. A groundbreaking ceremony was held in fall 1866 and construction commenced. Brown stone from southeast of Topeka was initially used for the east wing cornerstone and foundation construction.

That brown sandstone failed to harden; after a harsh winter in 1867 the stone had crumbled. Mudge selected much harder limestone from Geary County, which was light gray and buff, to replace the foundation and complete the wing. Stone from Cottonwood Falls was used for other portions of the building.

Much of the stonework was completed on location. Topekans commented that the sounds of the chipping of stone could be heard throughout the city. Considered complete in 1903, portions of the Capitol remained under construction until about 1917.

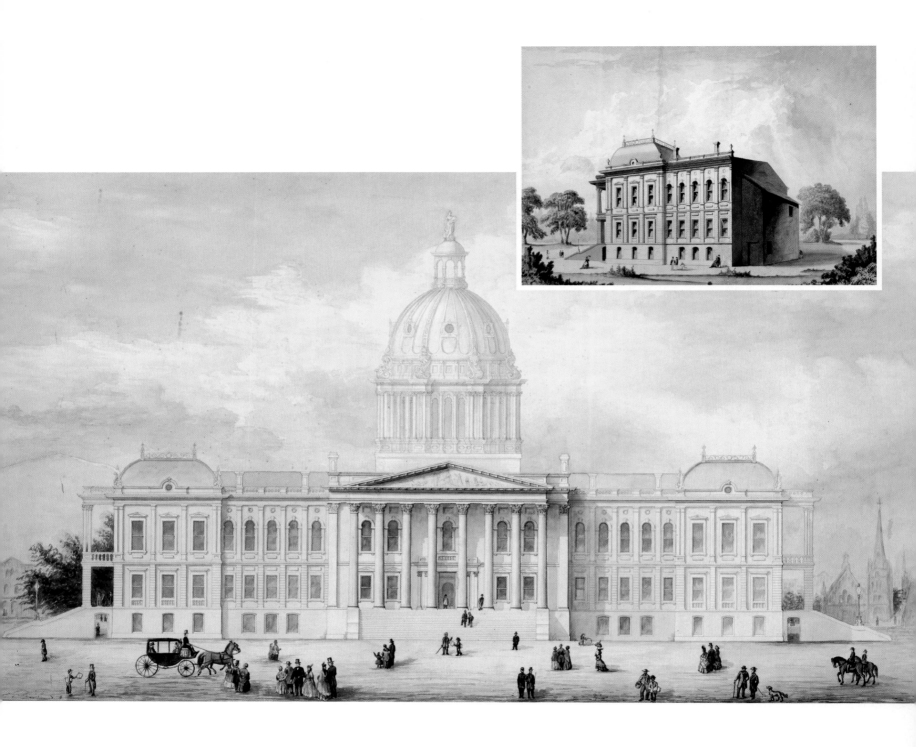

OPPOSITE TOP: This 1866 original concept for the east wing of the Capitol was designed by Mix.

OPPOSITE: This watercolor is one of Mix's original concepts for the Capitol, featuring classically-inspired design with Second Empire style influence with the steep mansard roof.

TOP: John Gideon Haskell of Lawrence is credited with the primary design of the Capitol. Pictured circa 1900, Haskell also was responsible for designing a number of courthouses in Kansas including those in Chase and Douglas counties, and many buildings on the University of Kansas campus.

ABOVE: Edward Townsend Mix of Wisconsin was the first architect hired to design the Capitol. This portrait is from the *National Cyclopedia of American Biography*, 1875-1879.

Kansas State Capitol
ARCHITECTS

In 1866 a design submitted by Edward Townsend Mix was authorized for the new state capitol. Mix, the state architect in Milwaukee, Wisconsin, proposed a concept that was classically influenced and encompassed more than 300,000 square feet. John G. Haskell of Lawrence was hired as statehouse architect. At the request of the building committee, Haskell modified the design to make the building more fire resistant, increase use of natural lighting, attach the wings similar to the U. S. Capitol, and incorporate heating and ventilation techniques more like monuments in the East. Haskell was authorized to explore other sites but to travel no farther East than Philadelphia. Both Haskell and Mix received credit for the design of the east wing. Haskell is credited with the design for the south wing, north wing, and main building.

Erasmus T. Carr of Leavenworth was hired as state architect in 1879 to oversee construction of the west wing. George Ropes of Lawrence, along with Carr, received credit for the design of the west wing.

Statehouse architects during construction

1866	Edward T. Mix
1866-1874	John G. Haskell
1874-1879	No architect
1879-1885	Erasmus T. Carr
1885-1886	John G. Haskell, Louis M. H. Wood
1886-1887	George C. Ropes
1887-1889	Kenneth McDonald
1889-1891	George C. Ropes
1891-1893	John G. Haskell
1893-1895	Seymour Davis
1895-1897	J. C. Holland
1897-1899	T. C. Lescher
1899-1909	John F. Stanton

CAVE OF THE WINDS

When Representative Hall opened in the west wing in 1881, a protective walkway was needed to connect the two wings. The chute or bridge provided access for messages to be carried from one legislative body to the other. The *Topeka Daily Capital* reported that the bridge was "suspended in the air connecting the two houses of the legislature."

Nicknamed the "Cave of the Winds," this long narrow passage captured air flow as people walked through the tunnel, enhancing the Capitol's reputation as a "windy" place. The structure was demolished when construction began on the south and north wings and the main building.

A second passageway was built in 1888 to bypass the ongoing construction of the central building.

RIGHT: The west wing, at left, in 1880, is connected to the east wing by a covered walkway to protect people as they crossed between the two buildings.

TEAMS OF HORSES

The process of raising and lowering the huge building stones into place was accomplished early on through a pulley and hoist apparatus. Through repetitive motion, teams of horses passed backward and forward a distance of 75 yards, drawing a rope that turned a pulley. The hoist connected to the pulley carried the huge rock, mortar, and other building materials to the upper stories. A whistle from the foreman notified the driver of the team when to proceed forward or backward and when to stop. The horses became so accustomed to the repetition of the signals that they responded even without prompting.

LEFT: Teams of horses, pictured circa 1885, pulled wagons filled with cut limestone during the construction of the Capitol.

ABOVE: Foundation stones can be seen on the ground floor.

STONEMASON TOOLS

During the early construction limestone was carved onsite and positioned using horse-drawn cranes. Nels Ferguson was one of the stonemasons who carved the large stones. The Swedish immigrant, who worked for Tweeddale Construction, was a fixer mason who placed massive stones and applied mortar. He used the level and plumb bob to ensure proper alignment, and the crowbar for leveraging stones into position. The hand float may have been used to smooth the mortar between layers.

> *The south side of the State House yard is filled with stone,*
> *and the stone cutters' hammers make a merry music which*
> *may be heard some distance off . . . the outlines of the structure*
> *begin to show themselves.*
>
> —*Lawrence Daily Journal,* 1879

Ferguson had recently emigrated from Sweden when he went to Topeka. There he met his new wife and began working on the statehouse. During the multiyear restoration, two state legislators, Elaine Bowers and Mark Taddiken, purchased the tools and donated them to the Historical Society.

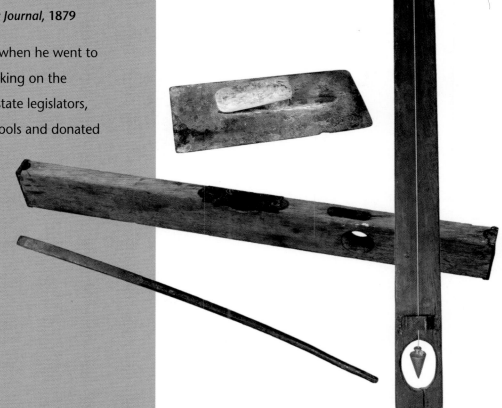

RIGHT: Nels Ferguson used these tools in his work as a stonemason on the Capitol, clockwise from top right, plumb bob, tamping bar, mason's level, and float.

The stonemasons who cut and shaped the limestone for the Capitol pose on the south steps in 1888.

ELECTRIC DERRICK

As construction continued on the upper floors of the Capitol, the horsepower used to move heavy building materials was replaced by newer technologies. Newspapers of the day claimed the "first ever built" electric derrick was installed in 1886. The tall tower and electric motor were placed between the south and west wings. Developed by George H. Evans and Company of Topeka, the lift from the electric motor assisted with hoisting heavy stone and other materials where workers could install them in the exterior and interior.

RIGHT: Workers can be seen on the ground and atop the Capitol near the electric derrick in 1886. The derrick was removed by the early 1890s.

Temporary buildings and construction materials fill the grounds of the Capitol in 1886, with the electric derrick standing near the main building between the south and west wings. Harrison Street is pictured in the foreground; an early Santa Fe office building stands to the right behind the Capitol.

DANGER

Hundreds of laborers participated in the construction of the Capitol; nine men gave the ultimate sacrifice in the process of its completion. Andrew Petersen was struck a fatal blow in 1888 by a crank while hoisting the huge foundation stones. John Cane was working on the top most part of the dome in 1890 when he lost his balance and fell 130 feet to his death. Some men were more fortunate. Will Ransom was working on the fourth floor rotunda in 1888 when he fell 72 feet to the ground floor. He claimed he was unhurt.

LEFT: Nine men were killed during the construction including John Cane, an ironworker who fell from the dome to his death. The dome ironwork is pictured in 1893.

CLASSICALLY INSPIRED

Classical architecture in Greece, Rome, and Europe commonly influenced building styles in the United States. The design of the U. S. Capitol was no exception and influenced the plans proposed by Edward Townsend Mix.

John G. Haskell, the statehouse architect, was asked to revise the design. His version also incorporated classically-inspired elements, which became the design constructed. He changed the placement of the wings and interior and removed the mansard roof. Haskell proposed the shape of a Greek cross, with magnificent colonnades at the end of each arm. The exterior of each wing would feature finely cut masonry with a rougher outer surface, a smooth middle section, and classical detail above the columns. The building roof would be made of copper. His revisions were approved by the Capitol building committee.

Most of the windows have cut limestone sills and lintels. The east and west wings have arched windows; the designs for these windows are distinctly American, an adaptation of the Italian arched window used in the Victorian period in America.

Sculptures were to be etched in the north and south pediments above the columns. The building committee planned for the spaces to "embrace the characteristic features of the great seal of the state," according to the *Topeka Daily Capital*, April 6, 1890, and be "devoted entirely to the representation of the central and always most memorable and most noble era of Kansas political history, the struggle between slavery and freedom." Architect George Ropes submitted a design for the south pediment. This project was never completed and the irregular stones on the pediments are still visible today.

Haskell planned a dome similar to that of the U. S. Capitol, one that would include a statue on top, plus others throughout the building. George Evans, the contractor for the dome, expressed his personal sentiments regarding Haskell's use of classical precedents. "I believe that we have not got far away enough from the old Greek and Egyptian models," he said.

ABOVE: The detailed capitals atop fluted columns were inspired by early Greek and Roman architecture.

OPPOSITE: The south wing is pictured at night in 1947.

People cross 9th Avenue and Jackson Street near the east wing of the Capitol in 1898.

Kansas State Capitol
EAST WING

German masons completed the stonework for the east wing, which was finished in 1873. The total cost of construction for the east wing was reported at $480,000.

The east and west wings were made similar in detail with 34 steps leading to the six Corinthian columns, classical railing on the roof, and double door entrance to the second floor. The wings feature different window types—flat arched windows on the first floor and full arched windows on the second floor. The east wing is shorter and narrower than the west wing.

The east wing was the largest building in the state at the time of its completion. State government offices moved from various temporary locations to the new space in December 1869, while it was yet under construction. The Supreme Court was located on the first floor of the east wing. The governor, secretary of state, auditor, treasurer, superintendent of public instruction, and attorney general offices were located on the second floor. Both bodies of the state legislature met on the third floor; a wall separated the chambers.

In the temporary wooden steps which have been put up at the east front, the visitor perceives a remarkable resemblance to the "shoot" up which the pigs march to certain death in a slaughterhouse. Having surmounted this architectural triumph, the visitor finds himself in the central hall on the second floor of the building.

—**Kansas State Record**, Topeka, December 22, 1869

The east wing was remodeled in 1885 after the west wing was completed, and the ornate Senate Chamber was created.

A characteristic unique to the east wing is its size, four feet narrower and six feet shorter than the west wing. A fountain was once located near the east steps, pictured in 1888. This fountain may have come from the Kansas display at the 1876 Philadelphia Exposition.

Kansas State Capitol
WEST WING

Like the east wing, the west wing features six Corinthian capitals crowning the columns. The door at the top of the flight of 34 stairs enters at the second floor. Work on the west wing began in 1879, with Italian masons involved in construction. The building was enclosed by 1880. Work was still underway when the Kansas House of Representatives first met in the hall in 1881. The wing was finished by the end of the year. The total cost of construction for the wing was reported at $317,000.

A visit to the upper stories of the building at present reveals a busy-scene, in which is mingled carpenters, masons, steam-fitters, plumbers and gas-fitters, all busy as bees, putting in the temporary fittings and furnishings, to be in readiness for the legislature by the 10th of January.
—Topeka Daily Commonwealth, December 24, 1880

Representative Hall, the larger of the two chambers, contains space for the 125 members. The hall is also used during joint sessions, such as the governor's annual state of the state address.

OPPOSITE: The west wing is pictured at night in 1948.

ABOVE: Characteristics unique to the west wing are a cross-like pattern on the second floor and keystone detail in the door arch.

The south wing of the Capitol is pictured circa 1910, with trees lining the driveway. By 1906 the oxidation process had begun to turn the copper on the roof and dome green. Characteristics of the south wing include eight fluted columns topped with capitals and two arched doors.

Kansas State Capitol
SOUTH WING

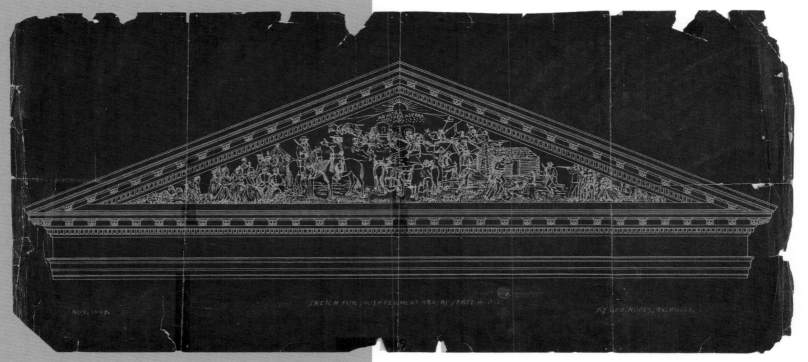

Construction on the south wing began in 1883, along with work on the north wing. Portions of the wing were occupied as early as 1892. Unique to the south wing are the two doors at the top of the staircase leading to the second floor. Once the city grew beyond the downtown area to the north, many activities were held on the lawn near the south wing.

The third floor of the south wing contains the Old Supreme Court; the restored space is now one of several large committee rooms. The fifth floor was once home to the Kansas Historical Society.

The south pediment of the Capitol was left rough in anticipation of a frieze that would be added to the stone.

The original plans for the north and south wings included a relief design on the pediments above the columns. This design by George Ropes, statehouse architect, was planned for the south pediment.

The state seal and state motto, *Ad astra per aspera* (to the stars through difficulties), were adopted through a joint resolution during the first Kansas legislative session on May 25, 1861. The design of the seal, which includes 34 stars representing Kansas' entry as the 34th state in the Union, was originally submitted by John J. Ingalls, a U. S. senator from Atchison, but was significantly modified by members of the state legislature.

Kansas State Capitol
NORTH WING

Construction on the north wing began in 1883 along with work on the south wing. The main building construction began in 1886, and construction on the dome began in 1889. These sections were generally completed in 1903, however, the north portico construction continued until 1906. The north wing, designed as the front door, features special details including three exterior doors with the Kansas state seal made of copper inlay, and the eight fluted columns consistent with the south wing.

The State Library of Kansas is located on the third and fourth floors of the north wing. The secretary of state's office, originally located in the northeast corner of the wing, was moved to Memorial Hall in 2000. The original space is used today as a ceremonial office.

In 1947 state legislators made the south wing the official entrance. The multiyear restoration once again returns that function to the north wing.

OPPOSITE: People crowd the steps of the north wing of the Capitol in 1904 shortly after the official completion of construction. An early Santa Fe office building can be seen to the left behind the Capitol.

LEFT: Characteristics of the north wing include the three arched doors with keystones atop the arches and other ornamental details. The three doors have copper inlay featuring the state seal.

DOME STATUE

Ceres, the Roman goddess of agriculture, was the first choice for the statue to be mounted atop the Capitol dome. In 1890, when Capitol construction was nearing completion, design submissions were requested. J. H. Mahoney of Indianapolis was chosen and the firm prepared a plaster model of the goddess. The cost estimate for the bronze statue was $6,950. Concerns grew about the subject and the financial commitment for the statue and the project was cancelled. A light was the only adornment on the dome for many years.

The bronze statue of a Kansa warrior was placed on top of the dome in 2002. Sculpted by Salina artist Richard Bergen, *Ad Astra* stands 22 feet and 2 inches tall and weighs 4,420 pounds. Steel plates were bolted in place to stabilize the statue from the wind. The warrior faces toward the North Star, a symbol of finding one's way. Specially designed lighting makes for a dramatic view of the statue at night.

RIGHT: The statue of the Kaw warrior was named after the state motto: *Ad astra per aspera,* "to the stars through difficulties."

RIGHT: A bronze statue of Ceres, the Roman goddess of agriculture, created by John F. Stanton, statehouse architect, was originally planned to top the Capitol. This plaster model, created in 1890, reflects the proposal for the design.

BELOW: Lumen Martin Winter proposed this concept for a statue of an American Indian to top the dome. His design included removing a portion of the dome above the cupola to accommodate the statue, *Topeka Daily Capital*, January 19, 1953.

FACTS

Numerous other statues were planned for the Capitol. Four were to be located on pedestals at the north entrance, two at the top of the two main gables, and eight sitting statues above the columns. None of these was completed. Several famous or fictional Kansans were considered for the four statues in the marble niches in the second floor rotunda including John Brown, James Lane, Carry Nation, and a jayhawker. A nine-foot bronze statue of Cyrus K. Holliday was also envisioned for the grounds.

Kansas State Capitol
LANDSCAPING AND GROUNDS

Even before construction was underway on the Capitol, lawmakers were concerned about upkeep of the grounds. During the 1866 session, immediately after the Topeka Town Association had presented the 20 acres to the state, legislators voted to install a stone wall around the perimeter to protect against "village cows and other animals running over the townsite." Stones from a Topeka farm were used and laid by early settlers.

William Fernald was a young boy when the Capitol was under construction. He recalled that corn was planted there in 1867 and the grounds were filled with rabbits. A partially collapsed stone wall circled the grounds; the entrance was located near 9th Avenue and Harrison. A creek located near 3rd Avenue and Jackson provided water for the workhorses, which boys carried in buckets to the worksite.

In 1871 lawmakers hired landscape designer H. W. S. Cleveland and civil engineer William M. R. French to develop a landscape plan for Capitol Square. *Working Plans for Arranging the House Grounds* encompassed tree and shrub plantings and walkways in each quadrant. Although that plan was not implemented, the 1872 legislative session approved $8,000 to grade the land, replace the stone wall with a more attractive and secure "five-board, pig-tight fence," and to plant trees. William Tweeddale and Company conducted the plantings, which featured a row of elms planted along both 8th Avenue and Jackson. The trees were larger than normally transplanted and

nearly all died. As a result, a citizens group launched an Arbor Day celebration.

At the suggestion of many citizens who desire to see the capitol grounds made an ornament to the city, I hereby appoint Friday, April 23, 1875, as Arbor Day, and request all citizens on that date to set out trees in the capitol grounds. On that day, it is hoped that each citizen interested, will repair to the grounds, between the hours of 2 p. m. and 5 p. m., and set out one tree. The secretary of state will point out the proper locations for the trees.

—Thomas J. Anderson, mayor of Topeka

Volunteers planted 700 to 800 trees along the perimeter of the 20 acres that first year. In 1883 George W. Glick, the 9th Governor of Kansas, issued a proclamation designating April 25 as Arbor Day in Kansas. That tradition continues today.

LEFT: In April 2013 Governor Sam Brownback receives assistance in continuing the Arbor Day tradition by planting a tree on the Capitol grounds.

OPPOSITE: In 1875 the first Arbor Day celebration was made possible with volunteers who planted hundreds of trees. To the right of the east wing is the statehouse privy, which was removed during construction of the west wing; indoor accommodations were included in the building by the 1890s. Two other structures can be seen in the distance to the west of the Capitol.

SIDEWALKS

Governor Edmund Morrill was frustrated that he was unable to control people's natural desire to cross the grounds diagonally. In 1896 he announced that fines would be issued to those who varied from the sidewalk.

J. A. Dailey was a civil engineer who worked at the Santa Fe offices across the street on Jackson. He announced he would stage a protest, saying that he was merely crossing the grounds in a logical place. As D.C. Naylor, the police officer, was at his post, Dailey walked across the lawn one morning on the way to work. "But you can't cross these grounds," Naylor said. "I am going through this way or not at all," Dailey replied. Dailey was arrested and taken to the city prison. Diagonal sidewalks were eventually adopted on the grounds and are used today.

This illustration shows the path across Capitol Square taken by J. A. Dailey when he was arrested in 1896.

RIGHT: Edmund N. Morrill, the 13th Governor of Kansas, seated in his office, between 1895 and 1897.

OPPOSITE: The east wing of the Capitol in 1898 showing tree lined driveways, paved walkways, and an unpaved diagonal path to the southeast similar to that advocated by Dailey.

The restored floor of Representative Hall and fourth floor gallery as it appears today.
©2013 Architectural Fotographics/Treanor Architects

Kansas State Capitol
HOUSE OF GOVERNMENT

The majestic Capitol has always been a place of pride for Kansans. The founders wanted this house of government to follow traditional designs, reflecting the hopes and beliefs of the state's citizens.

The building committee incorporated a number of innovations in the planning to ensure that the statehouse operated in an efficient manner and to safeguard their investment. They incorporated use of natural lighting throughout at the dawn of electrical lighting. They developed elements to resist fire in a time of coal heating when fires were fairly common threats to buildings and firefighting services were rare.

The 1909 Capitol floor plans list several offices on the first floor including that of the adjutant general. The second floor was home to several statewide elected officials. The governor and attorney general were in the south wing, the treasurer was in the west wing, the secretary of state was in the north wing. On the third and fourth floors were the Senate in the east, the House in the west, Supreme Court in the south, and the State Library in the north. On the fifth floor was the Kansas Historical Society's library in the south wing and museum in the north wing. This floor did not have the same level of finish work as the other floors.

TOP TO BOTTOM: A door knob, marble feature, and vent in the ornate grill in the Senate Chamber.

The Kansas legislature met in several places before completion of the Capitol, including Constitution Hall, pictured in 1879, located on the west near 5th and Kansas Avenue.

The legislature met in the Gale block, pictured between 1863 and 1865, in the 600 block on the east side of Kansas Avenue.

The legislature met in the Ritchie block, on the east side at 6th and Kansas Avenue. The block burned in 1869.

The east wing of the Capitol was still under construction when the legislature met in 1870. Taken from the southeast corner of the east wing circa 1870, workers and construction materials can be seen in the foreground.

Kansas State Capitol

FIRST LEGISLATIVE SESSION IN CAPITOL

The Kansas legislature convened its first meeting in the Capitol on January 11, 1870. Governor James Harvey delivered his address to the body beginning, "In the name of the people of Kansas, I welcome you, as their chosen law-giver, to these beautiful halls . . ." Eight thousand copies of his address were printed in English and 3,000 in German to be distributed to legislators and the public.

The House introduced several bills on its first day dealing with taxes, payment of county bonds, a county court of common pleas, repealing an act that would encourage growing hedges and building stone fences, and the establishment of highways through lands.

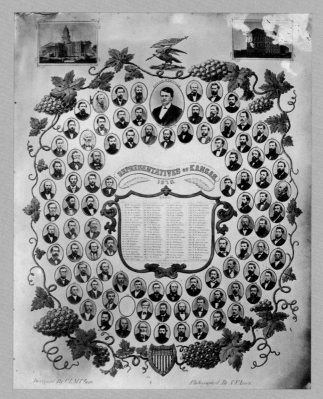

ABOVE: Members of the 1870 Kansas legislature.

RIGHT: *The Kansas House of Representatives Bills, 1870-1871.*

The Senate Chamber as it appeared after remodeling in 1886.

Kansas State Capitol
SENATE

The ornate Senate Chamber on the third floor of the east wing serves 40 senators who are elected every four years. During the first years of occupation when the east wing stood alone, the Senate and House shared the space on the third floor. In 1885, after the west wing was completed and the House moved out, the chamber was remodeled and the ornate plans for the room were finally implemented.

The unique design of the plaster ceiling was inspired by Egyptian architecture, Egyptian workers assisted with the update. The round windows originally featured a combination of prism and stained glass. A variety of marble can be seen in the chamber: gray blue marble on the lower wall from Belgium, onyx on the upper wall from Mexico, white marble above from Italy, and marble above the doors from Tennessee.

About 50 feet wide and 68 feet deep, the chamber features massive columns that were hand-cast in Italy. The hollow columns had ornate circular grills that encouraged air circulation. They could also be opened to allow hot air to rise to the attic. The desks made of native Kansas wild cherry wood, removed during earlier renovations, have been returned to their original place in the semicircle.

The *Topeka Daily Commonwealth* reported on January 17, 1886, that the new chamber appears "as if some fairy's magic wand had been waved over it and transformed it from the unsightly and uncomfortable old rookery that it was into the magnificent palace that it is."

LEFT: This small utilitarian green cart was used to deliver mail to state senators in the 1930s.

ABOVE: Columns, marble detail, and circular air vents can be seen looking to the back of the side aisle of the Senate Chamber. ©2013 Architectural Fotographics/Treanor Architects

OPPOSITE: Men are seated in the Senate Chamber in 1886.

OPPOSITE: The restored Senate Chamber as it appears today. ©2013 Architectural Fotographics/Treanor Architects

ABOVE: Bronze versions of the state seal above the doorways are among many details featured in the chamber.

Representative Hall was not yet complete when it opened in 1881. Floors, desks, and chairs were temporary and much of the final finish had yet to be applied. This view from 1899 shows the murals of St. Louis artist Ettore S. Miragoli on the ceiling and the chandeliers in place.

Kansas State Capitol
HOUSE OF REPRESENTATIVES

The House of Representatives is comprised of 125 members elected every two years from across the state. Representative Hall was designed especially for legislators and was first used during the 1881 session. Under construction at the time, the walls were not yet plastered and the floors were temporary.

Located on the third floor in the west wing, the hall is 73 feet wide and 34 feet high and features wainscoting of brown marble from Tennessee on the east wall, trimmed with Italian marble. The hall includes panels of Brocelian marble. Green Belgian marble was used on the column bases with faux marble above, in a process using plaster called scagliola. On top of the columns and on the ceiling is 22-karat gold leaf. The fourth floor gallery provides a viewing area for the public.

LEFT: This modified baby buggy was used for Jimmy Knight's vending service in the 1940s at the Capitol. A small propane tank could be attached to the outside as a fuel source to keep the chili hot.

ABOVE: These statehouse reporters, pictured in the press area near the front of Representative Hall, covered the news at the Capitol when officially completed in 1903.

OPPOSITE: The pink columns in the hall feature a faux marble plaster process called scagliola.

©2013 Architectural Fotographics/Treanor Architects

REPRESENTATIVE HALL ARTWORK

The *Topeka Commonwealth* reported in 1880 that Representative Hall would feature images of "Kansas men who have been prominent in the history of the State, and are now gone to their final rest," and that some might "cause controversy and even reopen old wounds."

Instead of images, the names of 10 prominent men were added above the windows. In 1908 artist and newspaperman Albert Reid covered the names with frescos. In 1998 the original works were uncovered and restored, revealing the 10 names.

Henry J. Adams	T. W. Barber
John Brown	M. F. Conway
Alfred Gray	J. H. Lane
J. Montgomery	Benj. F. Mudge
A. H. Reeder	C. Robinson

Murals were painted on the ceiling in 1882 by Ettore S. Miragoli of St. Louis. The murals are *Law* (above the desk of the speaker of the house and pictured below), to the left is *History*, to the right is *First Dawn of Liberty*, and above the main entrance is *Justice*.

The restored Representative Hall as it appears today. ©2013 Architectural Fotographics/Treanor Architects

The Republican-led House of Representatives assistants at arms pictured February 20, 1893, following a stand-off between Republicans and Populists.

Kansas State Capitol
LEGISLATIVE WAR

When the Kansas House of Representatives convened in 1893, two different parties claimed a majority. Elections were still being disputed and it was not immediately clear who had won the House. Populist Governor Lorenzo D. Lewelling and the Populist-controlled Senate recognized the Populist House as the official body. The Republicans and the Populists each elected their own officers and assigned their own committees.

For the next few weeks the two legislatures attempted to carry on their work while voters gathered in communities across Kansas to protest the dual bodies. When the Populists locked the Republicans out of Representative Hall, the Republicans used sledgehammers to break through the massive doors. They hired guards to secure the west wing and treasurer's office and sent the Populists to a separate statehouse room, with no electricity or telephone service.

Governor Lewelling requested support from the militia, which arrived from around the state to maintain order. He faced the dilemma of supporting his party while serving as commander of the peacekeeping troops. He brokered a deal that ultimately favored the Republicans, and the Kansas Supreme Court ruled in their favor. The lawmakers from both sides peacefully returned to complete the few remaining days of the legislative session.

ABOVE AND BELOW: The Republicans used sledgehammers, including this one, to break through the doors of Representative Hall when the Populists locked them out.

Advocates gathered on the north steps of the Capitol in 1916 to support the national amendment for full voting rights for women.

Kansas State Capitol
WOMEN'S SUFFRAGE

THE WESTERN UNION TELEGRAPH COMPANY

Some participants in the Wyandotte Constitutional Convention were leaders in supporting voting rights for women. Delegates included discussions about women's suffrage as the constitution was being debated. Although women were not permitted to be delegates, Clarina Nichols was allowed to address the convention in support of women's rights. The final version of the Wyandotte Constitution reflects Nichols' influence. It includes three provisions she championed: women's rights in child custody, married women's property rights, and equality in matters pertaining to public schools.

Legislators placed a constitutional amendment on the ballot in 1867 that would have granted equal suffrage to women and African Americans in Kansas. Although supported by the governor and female advocates like Susan B. Anthony and Elizabeth Cady Stanton, the vote failed. The 15th Amendment to the U. S. Constitution, passed two years later, gave voting rights to African American men.

In 1887 legislators passed a bill allowing women to run in municipal elections. That April women captured several local offices. They won all five seats on the Syracuse city council, and Susanna Madora Salter of Argonia was the first woman in the nation to be elected mayor.

In 1912 legislators once again placed on the ballot a constitutional amendment granting women the vote. On November 5, 1912, Kansas' male voters approved the Equal Suffrage Amendment. Kansas became the eighth state to grant full suffrage to women. Eight years later states ratified the 19th Amendment to the U. S. Constitution, giving women the right to vote.

TOP: Women and men formed the Kansas Equal Suffrage Association and finally gained full voting rights for women in the 1912 election. These women suffragettes were in Governor Walter Roscoe Stubb's automobile near the Capitol in 1912. First Baptist Church on Jackson Street and Santa Fe office building can be seen.

ABOVE: Supporters received this telegram of congratulations from a national women's organization after the successful passage of the 1912 state constitutional amendment.

The Supreme Court was remodeled in the 1930s when a wooden backdrop was added behind the bench. Several other modifications were made to the chamber, pictured in 1972.

Kansas State Capitol
OLD SUPREME COURT

Seven Supreme Court justices were seated at the bench in 1915.

The former Kansas Supreme Court chamber is located on the third floor of the south wing. Justices moved from the first floor of the east wing, to the first floor of the south wing, and finally to this chamber when it was completed in 1896.

In this chamber the court decided many significant cases including the 1925 ruling that made Kansas the first state to outlaw the Ku Klux Klan.

. . . the court will leave its quarters in the state capitol building with keen regret. It has been a cherished association and one replete with priceless memories.

**—Chief Justice Harold Fatzer
November 26, 1974**

In 1978 the Kansas Supreme Court moved to the Kansas Judicial Center located to the south of the Capitol. The legislature passed a resolution declaring the chamber's historic place in Kansas history and committing to preserve it for future generations. The chamber continues to be used for committee meetings. The Judicial Center houses the Kansas Supreme Court and the Kansas Court of Appeals.

CUSTODIAN AND ARTIST

L. D. Robinson was head custodian and an amateur artist in the 1930s. He created at least three pieces of artwork including a mural for the attorney general's office, a mural in Representative Hall, and a wood carving of the Supreme Court seal behind the justices' bench. Robinson had volunteered to make the carving when contractors expressed doubt about completing the project. With a piece of 18-inch ponderosa pine measuring two-and-a-half inches thick, Robinson created the piece in his spare time. This carving, now outside the Old Supreme Court, is his only remaining work on display at the Capitol.

L. D. Robinson created murals in several rooms in the Capitol.
Topeka State Journal, September 9, 1937

The Old Supreme Court as it appears today with chandeliers, stenciling, and oak details.
©2013 Architectural Fotographics/Treanor Architects

RIGHT: Located on the third floor in the north wing, construction of the State Library was underway in 1887.

BELOW: The State Library was completed in 1900 and included shelving and a mezzanine with glass flooring to maximize the flow of light, making it suitable for reading.

Kansas State Capitol
STATE LIBRARY OF KANSAS

Established by the first territorial legislature in 1855, the State Library was formerly located in the east wing of the Capitol. The library received its first state appropriation in 1863 to make it a depository of legal and historical documents and as a ready resource to the executive and legislative branches of Kansas government. When the north wing was completed in 1900, the library was moved there to its current site on the third and fourth floors. Designed especially for the library, the second deck features a glass floor made of 383 panes three-fourths of an inch thick designed to maximize the flow of light. The new library space was the first room in the Capitol to have electricity, which was installed throughout the entire building by 1911.

Today the library's functions have grown to serve the residents of Kansas through direct service and the support of local libraries.

The new rooms are not only spacious and commodious, but delightfully attractive as well. The frescoing is exquisite in color and the woodwork fine of finish...

—Annie Diggs, state librarian, 1900

TOP TO BOTTOM: Ornate stair railing, sunflower, and Corinthian columns accent the highly detailed State Library.

Annie Diggs

ABOVE: The State Library was completed in 1900 with two stories of shelving. A glass floor on the mezzanine was utilized to help maximize the flow of light for reading. ©2013 Architectural Fotographics/Treanor Architects

OPPOSITE: The restored State Library features ornate details on ceiling and columns along with decorative stenciling and iron balusters. ©2013 Architectural Fotographics/Treanor Architects

Kansas State Capitol
ROTUNDA

Much of the grandeur of the Capitol is created through the marble and carvings exhibited in the rotunda. The most colorful marble is located on the second floor. The rotunda, north wing, and south wing display panels of Rose St. Xavier and Rose deBrignoles marble wainscoting. The base and capstones are dark red marble from Belgium. The black-and-white marble throughout the building is from Georgia; the brown-colored marble from Tennessee; others types are from Italy and Mexico.

The interior dome is composed of an inner and outer section that extends to the ninth floor; the dome is about 67 feet in diameter. The glass panels of the inner dome can be viewed from below. Ornate brass columns on the sixth floor provide support for the dome. Decorative metal work above and below the columns is hand-hammered copper sheeting, and decorative panels extend to the upper rotunda. On the eighth floor is a catwalk, which leads to a spiral staircase, spanning approximately 75 feet between the tops of the inner and outer domes. The decorative cap above the inner dome allows the air to draw upward and ventilate the building. Clay or terra cotta tiles were used to line the inner dome, mortared in place with plaster.

In 1897 a 10-foot by 10-foot gas and electric chandelier was installed in the dome. Seldom used, the bronze and brass chandelier, weighing between 300 and 800 pounds, was removed in 1942 and donated to a scrap metal drive during World War II. A replica chandelier once again lights the rotunda.

ABOVE: Architectural details in the rotunda, left to right: the capital of a column, circular balustrade on the third floor, and a pediment on the fifth floor.

OPPOSITE: The rotunda looking up from first floor. ©2013 Architectural Fotographics/Treanor Architects

OFFICES

In 1896 offices were completed for the governor, secretary of state, state treasurer, and attorney general. Located on second floor, these offices were finished with oak floors, woodwork, and furniture. Some of the rooms featured fireplaces, hand-carved oak details, and washbasins. Most of the washbasins were removed by 1935.

The office of the governor and lieutenant governor today feature oak floors, woodwork, and historic furniture. Visitors can view ceremonial offices of the governor and secretary of state, along with the office of the lieutenant governor on tour today. The secretary of state's office relocated to Memorial Hall in 2000.

John W. Leedy, the 14th Governor of Kansas, is pictured circa 1897 after the second floor offices of statewide elected officials were completed.

ABOVE: The offices of the governor's staff now occupy the space where Governor Leedy is pictured. ©2013 Architectural Fotographics/Treanor Architects

RIGHT: Sam Brownback, the 46th Governor of Kansas, is seated in his office on second floor.

The secretary of state's office was formerly located on the second floor in the north wing. Typical of the other offices of statewide elected officials, it featured details like chandeliers and stenciling, pictured circa 1906. Today this room is used for receptions and ceremonial office space.

LEFT: The only remaining original washbasin can be seen today in the secretary of state's ceremonial office.

BELOW: When the offices of statewide elected officials were completed in 1896 newspapers highlighted the oak floors and hand-carved oak fireplace. The former secretary of state's office still displays these features and can be seen on tours.

KANSAS HISTORICAL SOCIETY

The Kansas Editors' and Publishers' Association formed the Kansas Historical Society in 1875 to collect newspapers and manuscripts on the territorial period. In 1879 the Historical Society was made trustee of the state's history. The organization's first home was a bookcase in the state auditor's office in the east wing. Offices moved to the west wing in 1881. By 1893 collections were also being stored in the basement. That year the legislature authorized three rooms in the south wing for the Historical Society, which was occupying more space than any of the other state agencies.

> *Kansas has the fullest collection ever made by any state in its early years, because this was the first Society that began its career by collecting and preserving every copy of every newspaper published in the state.*

> **—George Martin, secretary, Kansas Historical Society, 1900**

In 1905 the Kansas legislature established the Historical Society as the repository of official government records. The 1909 Capitol plans placed the Historical Society's library in the south wing and museum on the north wing of the fifth floor. Federal Civil War claims and state appropriations covered the cost of Memorial Hall, built to the east of the Capitol, which provided a new home for the Historical Society in 1914. In 1984 the Historical Society's Kansas Museum of History moved to lands in west Topeka. The agency's remaining divisions moved there in 1995.

BELOW: The Historical Society's newspaper filing room as it appeared in 1890. Located in several different rooms in the Capitol, the Historical Society moved to new quarters in Memorial Hall across the street.

Staff members of the Historical Society are pictured circa 1903.

Kansas entered the Union as the 34th state. The legislature passed House Bill 34 to build the Capitol. The state seal, featuring 34 stars, is displayed on the doors of Representative Hall, inside the Senate Chamber, in the governor's office, on bronze grates in the north and south wings, and on the state flags in the governor's office and the Old Supreme Court. There are 34 steps leading to the east and west wings. Each globe on the chandeliers in the Senate Chamber has 34 stars. By coincidence, a statue of Dwight D. Eisenhower, the 34th President of the United States, is located on the second floor rotunda.

TOP: Buttress arches, visible on ground level, were used to reinforce the walls of the east and west wings to prevent them from collapsing.

ABOVE: New office space on the ground floor was made possible during the restoration by lowering the floor two feet. The huge foundation stonework is now visible and provides distinctive features to the new space.

OTIS CAGE ELEVATOR

The cage elevator, installed in 1923 in the east wing, continues to be operated by a staff person. Unique today, cage elevators were once commonly seen in public buildings. The legislature in 1976 passed a resolution marking its historic value and committing to its maintenance. People can ride the elevator from first to fifth floor.

©2013 Architectural Fotographics/Treanor Architects

Tragic Prelude by John Steuart Curry, painted from 1938 to 1940 with oil and egg tempura on plaster, features abolitionist John Brown holding a Bible and a rifle.

Kansas State Capitol
ARTWORK

TOP TO BOTTOM: Crossman's Spanish-American War soldier, Miragoli's *History*, and Felton's White statue are among the artwork on display at the Capitol.

The Kansas State Capitol was always envisioned as a place to celebrate the state's history and cultural heritage. The building committee incorporated space to accommodate memorials to the state's history through statues, murals, frescos, and other artistic expressions. The artwork would tell the unique story of Kansas—a state founded on the cause of freedom.

Within these walls are examples of the finest expressions of public art in the nation. Some of this Capitol artwork is known worldwide. Murals are on display in the rotunda on first and second floors, in Representative Hall, and in the inner dome. Statues are located on the second floor rotunda, on the grounds, and atop the dome.

The history of the discussions about which artwork would be placed at the Capitol can be nearly as interesting as the works themselves. A fountain was planned for the first floor rotunda, but never completed. The dome statue was delayed for many years. Much of the planned artwork was completed; most of it is on display, some was removed and replaced. Plans continue for new works of art to further depict the state's fascinating past.

OPPOSITE: Curry indicates an artistic element of *Tragic Prelude* for a promotional photograph, circa 1941.

TOP TO BOTTOM: Jack rabbits in *Kansas Pastoral*; man with a covered wagon in *Tragic Prelude*; chickens and sheep on the farm in *Kansas Pastoral*.

Kansas State Capitol
CURRY MURALS

John Steuart Curry, a painter from Kansas, created the murals in the east and west wings on the second floor.

> *The theme I have chosen is historical in more than one sense . . .*
> *In great measure it is the historical struggle of man with nature.*
> *. . . It is my family's tradition and the tradition of a great*
> *majority of Kansas people.*
>
> **—John Steuart Curry**

Tragic Prelude, in the east wing, considered among the best of public art, features abolitionist John Brown. Rich in symbolism, the painting includes a tornado and prairie fires to represent the gathering storms of war. Critics at the time disliked the overall menacing effect of the mural.

Kansas Pastoral in the west wing offers an idyllic view of the agricultural state. Critics complained that the Hereford bull was misshapen and the nighttime prairie scene appeared to be an ocean.

> *I show the beauty of real things under the hand of a beneficent*
> *Nature . . . so that we, as farmers, patrons, and artists can shout*
> *happily together, "Ad Astra per Aspera."*
>
> **—John Steuart Curry**

Curry planned eight panels in the rotunda on the life of the homesteader. To make room for the murals he requested the removal of some marble panels. The request was denied. Amid the criticism and strained relationship, Curry refused to sign his work and returned to Wisconsin; the state in response withheld some of his compensation.

CURRY MURALS

Curry's *Tragic Prelude* includes a frontiersman, conquistador, and missionary. The frontiersman depicts the early settlement of Kansas as he stands over a slain bison with thundering herds of bison in the background. The conquistador is Francisco Vázquez de Coronado. He is shown with Franciscan missionary Padre Padilla and the Spanish explorers of 1541.

It is my hope to paint the American scene in a distinguished manner.

—John Steuart Curry

LEFT: Preliminary sketch of Coronado, late 1930s.

BELOW: Preliminary sketch of the frontiersman, Coronado, and Padilla, late 1930s.

RIGHT: The frontiersman, Coronado, and Padilla from *Tragic Prelude*.

BELOW LEFT: Main elements of *Tragic Prelude* are outlined on the walls in the east wing. Curry added handwritten notes to this photograph, 1939.

BELOW RIGHT: Preliminary work on the frontiersman painted on a wall, 1940.

CURRY MURALS

Curry's *Kansas Pastoral* is located in the second floor west wing. The mural covers three adjacent walls and depicts a family and their farm as dusk approaches the prairie.

In this comparatively quiet corridor is portrayed Kansas in the time of fruitful harvest.

—**John Steuart Curry**

RIGHT: Main elements of *Kansas Pastoral* are outlined on the walls in the west wing. Curry added handwritten notes to this photograph, 1939.

BELOW: *Kansas Pastoral*, showing farmer and controversial Hereford.

Kansas State Capitol
ROTUNDA STATUES

The second floor rotunda statues were created by Peter F. "Fritz" Felten, Jr., a native of Hays. Felton used limestone from southern Kansas for the four statues of accomplished Kansans. Installed in 1981, each sculpture weighs about 2,000 pounds.

ABOVE: A crane lifts *Amelia Earhart* to the second floor portico, 1981.

RIGHT: *Dwight David Eisenhower* is one of four statues set inside marble alcoves; Lumen Martin Winter murals adorn the adjacent walls.

Kansas State Capitol
WINTER MURALS

Lumen Martin Winter was selected to complete the artwork in the second floor rotunda to fill the space left vacant by John Steuart Curry. A sculptor, painter, and muralist, Winter grew up on a ranch near Larned. He painted his scenes with oil on canvas at his studio in New Mexico, avoiding the criticism that Curry endured during the painting process. In 1978 the paintings were installed and dedicated.

The Statehouse is like a permanent museum. The paintings there will be there for as long as there is a Kansas. And if you're a creative person you have to make a contribution. It's like you make a pact with God when you're a kid.

—Lumen Martin Winter

ABOVE: *Threshing*, located in the second floor rotunda, southwest corner.

RIGHT: Winter used the 12 colors of oil paint on the palette and the brushes to touch up the paintings after their installation.

Kansas State Capitol
OVERMYER MURALS

An illustrator, artist, and muralist, David H. Overmyer of Topeka
gained recognition with his murals at Kansas State University and
Topeka High School. At the Capitol he pictured significant events in
Kansas history, painted directly onto the plaster walls.

Overmyer's *Battle of Arikaree* on the left and *Battle of Mine Creek* on the right, located in the
first floor rotunda, southeast corner. ©2013 Architectural Fotographics/Treanor Architects

Kansas State Capitol
DOME MURALS

Jerome Fedeli, a skilled Italian fresco painter, was hired in 1898 during a time of Populist control to create murals for the inner dome. Fedeli's design featuring Grecian women came under attack two years later when the Republican Party returned to power. In 1901 the *Topeka Daily Capital* called the figures "thinly clad telephone girls."

The Fedeli murals were replaced in 1902 with four allegorical murals by Abner Crossman of Chicago. Each scene was done on canvas and cut and fitted onto the curved soffit. The fresco between scenes was painted directly onto the plaster. The firm also designed the semi-relief statues and state seals located below the paintings.

The east panel features Knowledge in the center with Temperance on her left and Religion on her right. The south panel shows Power in the center with a sword in her hand; a Spanish-American War soldier is on her left and a Civil War Union soldier on her right. The west panel has Peace in the center with a sheathed sword; Science is on her left and Art on her right. The north panel shows Plenty in the center with labor on her left and Agriculture on her right.

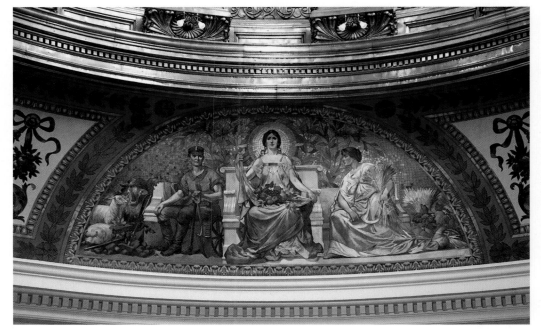

ABOVE: Fedeli's murals were on display in the dome, 1902.

RIGHT: Crossman's north panel mural as it appears today.

Kansas State Capitol
STAINED GLASS

In 1976 Americans celebrated the 200th anniversary of the founding of the United States. Two stained glass windows were donated by the Kansas Chapter of the Veterans of Foreign Wars. The windows can be seen in the south wing above the doors on the second floor. They were designed and created by Patrick C. McKinney, a Topeka artist, known for his stained glass works in public buildings, churches, and homes. Draped with an American flag, the window on the left depicts an American soldier in uniform flanked by a veteran, a soldier leading a charge, and a young man. The window on the right shows General George Washington during the American Revolution.

The two stained glass windows were installed during the U. S. Bicentennial in 1976.

TOP: Stenciling on the ceiling of the governor's conference room.

ABOVE, LEFT TO RIGHT: Staircase railing bracket, column and ceiling in the State Library, radiator in the Old Supreme Court.

Kansas State Capitol
FEATURES

Throughout the building are symbols inspired by the state's heritage. Sunflowers and the initials KS appear on brass railings. Intricate stencil borders were used on the walls and ceilings.

CLOCKWISE, FROM TOP RIGHT: Stained glass Senate window, wall art in Senate Gallery, keystone in arched Senate entryway, column in the Senate Chamber; newel at bottom of south wing staircase.

The south wing of the Capitol, 1979.

Kansas State Capitol
CAPITOL SQUARE

The 20-acre Capitol Square was fenced with stone when the Capitol was under construction. The stone was later replaced with a wooden fence to keep out feral animals. As the Capitol building grew nearer to completion, the public and legislators developed expectations for the appearance of the grounds. Tree planting efforts were undertaken, landscaping, sidewalks, and fountains were discussed.

The park-like setting became a gathering place for special events. Over the years numerous governors' inaugurations have been held on the grounds. It is the site of presidential visits, campaign launches, rallies, and celebrations. Many markers and memorials are located along the walkways to designate important people and events in the state's history.

TOP TO BOTTOM: Stone fountain on west lawn; exterior entry to ground level, north wing; capital at top of pilaster on west wing.

Kansas State Capitol
COTTONWOOD TREE

Legends surrounded the origin of the cottonwood tree that was a prominent feature for many years south of the Capitol. Some said the tree sprouted from construction stakes. T. J. Anderson, a former state adjutant general, provided an account in 1909 to the Kansas Historical Society. As construction began on the east wing Anderson noticed a small sapling growing between some of the large stones. He drove large stakes around the sapling to protect it. He and artist Henry Worrall took an interest in preserving the tree during construction, and it thrived over the years.

In 1882 the tree was damaged in a fire when a shed that had been a shelter to workmen caught fire and the tree was badly scorched. These marks were evident throughout the tree's life.

The 1966 Topeka tornado caused further damage to the old tree. In 1983 an effort was made to save the cottonwood. Large limbs on the 90-foot cottonwood were supported by wires attached to the 15-foot circumference of the trunk. Age, illness, and wind finally felled the cottonwood tree in 1984. Cuttings were taken from it and today a descendant of the original tree grows at the location of its ancestor.

ABOVE: The stately cottonwood tree on the Capitol grounds as it appeared in the 1940s. The tree was located in the southeast quadrant.

LEFT: The cottonwood sustained damage over the years including a lightning strike. During renovation in 1983 it was finally removed.

Kansas State Capitol
GAGE STATUES

Robert Merrell Gage of Topeka created two sculptures on the south lawn of the Capitol. In the southeast quadrant is the statue *Abraham Lincoln*. The sculpture, begun in 1916, was Gage's first public commission. Gage's work with Lincoln continued with his 1956 film, *The Face of Lincoln*, showing a wet clay bust that changed during the years of his presidency, earning him an Academy Award.

The memorial dedicated to the pioneer women of Kansas was finished in 1937. The Kansas Pioneer Women's Association raised funds for the sculpture during its 1927 membership drive; anyone who contributed $1 or more to the project was granted membership.

BELOW: The pioneer women memorial, created by Robert Merrell Gage, is located in the southwest quadrant.

RIGHT: *Abraham Lincoln*, also created by Gage, was begun in 1916 and is located in the southeast quadrant.

ABOVE: The Kansas Law Enforcement Memorial, located in the northeast quadrant, was dedicated in 1987 and honors Kansas law enforcement officials killed in the line of duty. A memorial to honor Kansas firefighters whose lives were lost in the line of duty in service to the state is planned to be installed nearby.

RIGHT: The Veterans Memorial, located to the south of the Capitol, was dedicated in 1997 and honors Kansans who have served, are serving, or will serve in the armed forces.

ABOVE: The Kansas Walk of Honor, located along walkways to the north and south, was dedicated in 2011 with Senator Bob Dole as the first honoree. The walk honors Kansans who have contributed on a state and national level.

RIGHT: The Statue of Liberty, located in the northwest quadrant, was dedicated in 1950, one of 200 donated by the Boy Scouts of America in celebration of the organization's 40th anniversary.

The Topeka public library, jointly funded by the Santa Fe Railway and Union Pacific Railway, was located on the grounds northeast of the Capitol. The building opened in 1883 and featured a performance stage. In 1953 the library was moved to a new building at 10th and Washburn, where it is still located today. The original library building was finally razed in 1961.

Parker Shows of Leavenworth featured a fair on the statehouse grounds in 1904
in celebration of the semi-centennial of Kansas Territory. Courtesy C.W. Parker
Archives/Collection of Barbara Fahs Charles

President William Howard Taft addressed a large audience from the south side in 1911. The 27th President of the United States was in Topeka to mark the state's 50th anniversary by laying the cornerstone of the Grand Army of the Republic Memorial Hall, which would be built to the southeast of the Capitol.

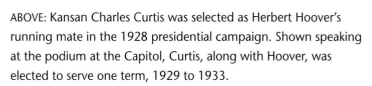

ABOVE: Kansan Charles Curtis was selected as Herbert Hoover's running mate in the 1928 presidential campaign. Shown speaking at the podium at the Capitol, Curtis, along with Hoover, was elected to serve one term, 1929 to 1933.

LEFT: Gerald Ford, the 38th President of the United States, addressed the Kansas legislature in 1975 and spoke to a gathering outside from the south steps.

LEFT: Members of Marshall's Band of Topeka gather on the north steps of the Capitol, circa 1900.

BELOW: Members of the Farmers Educational and Cooperative Union gather on the north steps of the Capitol, 1915.

OPPOSITE: G. D. Steen photographed an unidentified woman on the south portico, 1904. An early Santa Fe Railway office building is in the background.

The west wing of the Capitol is covered with scaffolding during the multiyear restoration effort from 1999 to 2014.

Kansas State Capitol
RESTORATION

Paint analysis was conducted and revealed several layers of paint as well as historic stenciling. Many uncovered stencils were restored.

The *Topeka State Journal* in 1936 estimated that the Capitol's lifespan was about 80 years and it would need to be replaced by 1986. Through the legislature's ongoing investment in maintenance, the Capitol's usefulness will extend far into the future.

Renovation has occurred numerous times in the building's history with an average of $200,000 per year spent on stone repair over the last few decades. Major appropriations were made in 1917 and 1948, with ongoing work from 1965 to 1974. The damage done during the 1966 Topeka tornado resulted in costly repairs.

These remodeling efforts over the years greatly changed the appearance of the building. The original use of skylight was changed with remodeling, subdividing, and drop ceilings, which darkened the building. Historic features had been altered, obscured, and removed.

By the end of the 20th century, portions of the statehouse were in poor condition. The mechanical and electrical systems needed updating, parking and safety were concerns. A multiyear restoration project began in 1999 to return the Capitol to its original grandeur and preserve it for the next century.

CAPITOL RESTORATION TIMELINE

Workers repair the damage to the dome from the 1966 Topeka tornado. Courtesy *Topeka Capital-Journal*

1966

Otis cage elevator is installed in east wing

Multiyear renovation includes work in Supreme Court chamber, exterior repairs

Remodeling adds offices, restrooms, lounges, meditation room

Dome reopens to public

1923   1948   1959   1963

1917   1935   1954   1961   1965

Repairs to east wing include deteriorated stone and office remodeling

Renovation includes removing washbasins in offices

Renovation work includes window replacement in dome

Dome closed to the public for repairs

Work includes repairing copper roof, restoring Curry murals

1917

Architects discuss the remodeling of the east wing offices.

1990

Workers excavate north steps

Metal restoration in south wing. Courtesy Treanor Architects

2008

Repairs to dome and roof damaged by tornado

Renovation begins on north steps

Multiyear restoration begins

Copper roof replacement begins

1966

1990

1999

2012

1976

1993

2002

2014

Repairs to Otis cage elevator

Minor renovation in Representative Hall

Construction begins on parking garage and vaults

Multiyear restoration ends

Steel plates added for wind stabilization in preparation of *Ad Astra* statue

2002

An aerial view of earth removal for parking garage. Courtesy Treanor Architects

"DISGRACE"

Throughout the construction process and just after completion, concerns emerged about the maintenance of the Capitol and the surrounding grounds. In the 1880s and 1890s it was a "health hazard" with pigs and cattle grazing on the grounds, "unsightly sheds," and "wretched" lawns according to the *Topeka State Journal*; in 1906 it was "greenish brown" dome, "shabby" statehouse steps, and dead and "withered" flowers. By 1917 some legislators claimed the statehouse was so disgraceful "self respecting farmers . . . wouldn't keep their cattle in it." In addition, the coal smoke from the boilers was blackening the limestone exterior.

OPPOSITE: The west wing appears overgrown, as the Capitol was draped in mourning cloth for the death of Ulysses S. Grant, the 18th President of the United States, who died on July 23, 1885.

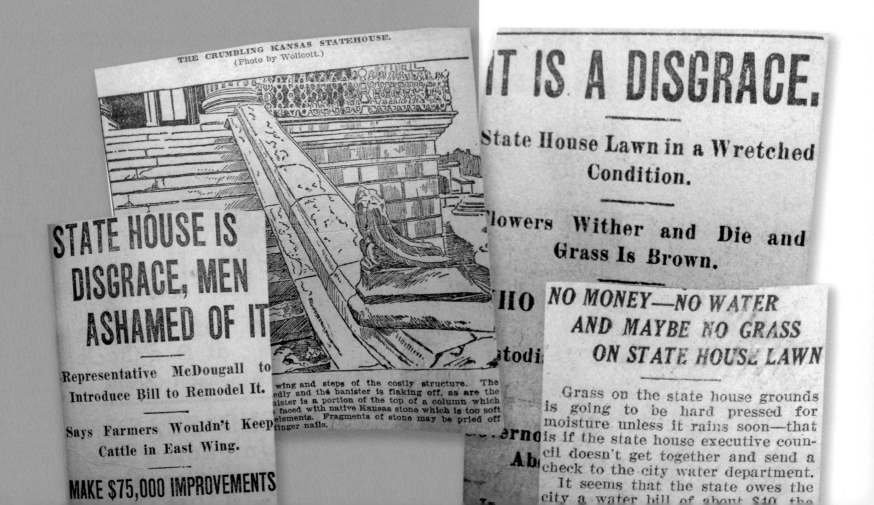

THE CRUMBLING KANSAS STATEHOUSE.
(Photo by Wollcott.)

IT IS A DISGRACE.

State House Lawn in a Wretched Condition.

Flowers Wither and Die and Grass Is Brown.

STATE HOUSE IS DISGRACE, MEN ASHAMED OF IT

Representative McDougall to Introduce Bill to Remodel It.

Says Farmers Wouldn't Keep Cattle in East Wing.

MAKE $75,000 IMPROVEMENTS

wing and steps of the costly structure. The
edly and the banister is flaking off, as are the
nister is a portion of the top of a column which
faced with native Kansas stone which is too soft
elements. Fragments of stone may be pried off
finger nails.

NO MONEY—NO WATER AND MAYBE NO GRASS ON STATE HOUSE LAWN

Grass on the state house grounds is going to be hard pressed for moisture unless it rains soon—that is if the state house executive council doesn't get together and send a check to the city water department.

It seems that the state owes the city a water bill of about $40 the

Kansas State Capitol
1966 TORNADO

In 1966 a tornado struck Topeka, which caused immense damage in the capital city. The mile-wide tornado was on the ground beyond the borders of the city from southwest to northeast, damaging homes, businesses, and downtown Topeka.

The Capitol was in the tornado's path. Many trees on the grounds were destroyed, and buildings surrounding the Capitol were heavily damaged.

The dome took the brunt of the storm's force. Flying debris punctured the copper on the dome and roof, causing damage totaling $157,121. Even after the repair, that portion of the dome would remain discolored as a reminder of the tragic storm.

The tornado was later determined to be an F5, with winds in excess of 260 miles per hour. It cut a four-block wide and eight-mile long swath, resulting in the deaths of 16 people, and more than $104 million in damage.

OPPOSITE: The black tornado funnel approaches a residential neighborhood in southwest Topeka, June 8, 1966.

TOP TO BOTTOM: Looking to the northwest, the impact of tornado damage to cars, trees, and buildings can be seen between Jackson Street and Kansas Avenue near 12th Avenue. Work is underway to repair the damage to the dome and west wing roof.

Kansas State Capitol
MULTIYEAR RESTORATION

The multiyear restoration of the Capitol began in 1999 and concludes in 2014. A major goal for the restoration, in addition to addressing exterior and interior deterioration, was to honor the Capitol's original appearance between 1903 and 1917.

Additional goals were to increase efficiency of space, provide for current and future energy and technology needs, and add parking, while continuing to conduct the state's business. Construction ceased in the areas where lawmakers worked during each legislative session.

The project added 118,000 square feet of space, for a total of 500,000 square feet. Much of the increase was achieved by lowering the floor two feet on the ground level creating 29,103 square feet of new space for offices and visitors. Four mechanical vaults were created underground in the four quadrants to reclaim 61,918 square feet on the ground floor. The new underground parking garage, to the north of the Capitol, offers 551 stalls on two levels and provides easy access to the Capitol entrance on the north.

Office spaces throughout the building, which had been heavily modified and sectioned over time, were restored to their original appearance. To improve traffic flow and accessibility, elevators and stairs were added.

Paint, stenciling, and trim were restored to their original appearance. Bronze and brass fixtures were restored and polished to their original sheen. The restoration also returned the extensive use of natural light throughout the building.

In Representative Hall new desks and chandeliers were installed to be consistent with original designs, and electronic voting boards replaced the older intrusive boards used in the late 20th century.

Exterior restoration included hand carving, stone stabilization, crack repair, patching, repainting, and stone cleaning. The copper sheeting on the dome and roof were among the last projects to be completed.

The Capitol was crumbling around our ears. There were unsafe wires, no sprinkling system. The heating system was archaic. It was just falling apart.

—Senate President Dick Bond, 1999-2000

I think this is a place that Kansans should be proud to come visit.

—Speaker of the House Robin Jennison, 1999-2000

OPPOSITE: Workers replace grill work over the door between the governor's office and conference room. Courtesy Treanor Architects

ABOVE: Capitol construction crews pose on the south steps while scaffolding covers the columns.

Ad Astra can be seen atop the Capitol while scaffolding covers the dome. At 340 feet, the huge
Comansa crane is the tallest free-standing tower crane in North America.

Workers install new copper on the dome.

ABOVE: An artist completes gold leaf on detailing in the Senate Chamber.

OPPOSITE TOP TO BOTTOM: Restoration of the ceiling in the Senate Chamber. Courtesy
Treanor Architects; the floor of the Senate Chamber is prepared for reinstallation of the desks
in a semicircular pattern. Courtesy Treanor Architects

LEFT: Workers restore woodwork in the old secretary of state's office. Courtesy Treanor Architects

BELOW: Stencils are uncovered in a subcommittee room on the second floor. Courtesy Treanor Architects

ABOVE: Scaffolding is in place in the inner dome during replacement of the copper exterior.

RIGHT: Restoration of the rotunda on the second floor.
Courtesy Treanor Architects

FOUND DURING RENOVATION

A number of interesting items were uncovered throughout the building, including a pair of rubber galoshes. A wood cylinder believed to be an original relief vent for the boiler was found at ground level in the main building. Several objects were found tucked into the lantern house during dome restoration, which include a letter in a copper envelope, business card, a tube of lipstick, a pocket knife, a 1916 Lincoln penny, and a tobacco pouch.

OPPOSITE: Crossman's north panel dome mural, with Plenty, Labor, and Agriculture, displays a tear prior to restoration. Courtesy Treanor Architects

ABOVE: Workers restore the inner dome. Courtesy Treanor Architects

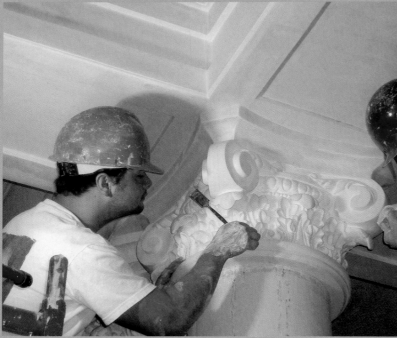

OPPOSITE: Workers create a new plaster capital for a column. Courtesy Treanor Architects

RIGHT: New construction of the southwest staircase between fourth and fifth floors.
Courtesy Treanor Architects

Capitol Square is covered in snow in this 1935 aerial. The Masonic Grand Lodge is to the northwest, Assumption Church is to the northeast, at the top. First Baptist Church, Santa Fe offices, and Memorial Hall are to the east, at the right. The Masonic Temple and state printer are located to the southeast, at the bottom. A residential area west of the Capitol, to the left, includes the Dillon House.

Kansas State Capitol
NEIGHBORHOOD

The neighborhood surrounding Capitol Square has changed considerably since the construction began on the grounds in 1866. Bordered on the north by 8th Avenue, on the south by 10th Avenue, on the east by Jackson Street, and on the west by Harrison Street, Capitol Square has been surrounded by farms, houses, churches, businesses, and state office buildings over the years.

G. D. Steen was an amateur photographer who lived in Topeka. In 1904 Steen took his camera to the top of the dome and completed a series of photographs from the cupola showing the neighborhood surrounding Capitol Square. Steen's revealing photographs capture a moment in time when the magnificent building had just been completed. Trolleys and carriages were the modes of transportation, many of the streets were unpaved, and houses filled the immediate neighborhood.

TOP TO BOTTOM: Residence on Harrison Street, between 8th and 10th avenues; the Oakland and State House trolley was electric and operated by the Topeka Rapid Transit Company, shown between 1885 and 1895; residence at 10th Avenue and Van Buren Street, circa 1880s.

NORTH

In 1866 the city of Topeka was located to the north and east of the statehouse. As the city grew, it expanded to the south and west, eventually surrounding the 20-acre tract. The Masonic Grand Lodge was built northwest of the Capitol on 8th Avenue, which later became the Kansas Highway Association building. Assumption Church was built to the north in 1862. The original church faced east, but when a new church was built on the site in 1882, it faced south toward the Capitol. The third church, built in 1924, is known today as Mater Dei Catholic Church. The parish school was built to the east in 1939. The Topeka Library was built on the northeast quadrant in 1883 where it stood until 1961; a new facility had opened several blocks west in 1953.

G. D. Steen, pictured at right in 1904, captured this image from the cupola of the dome looking north in 1904. The city library can be seen bottom right, along 8th Avenue, an east-west street, across from Assumption Church. A trolley car and horse and carriage travel along 8th through a residential area. The county courthouse can be seen at the top center along Van Buren, a north-south street.

RIGHT: View north of the Capitol as it appears today with the Kansas Highway Association at the west and Mater Dei at right.

EAST

The Atchison, Topeka & Santa Fe Railway office building, which opened in 1884, was located to the east of the statehouse on Jackson Street. A new building was constructed to the south in 1910 and the remaining structure was replaced in 1924. It was dedicated the Landon State Office Building in 1985 to honor the presidential candidate and 26th Governor of Kansas, Alfred M. Landon. The First Baptist Church, located north of the Santa Fe offices, was built in 1876 where it remained until 1970, when the church moved south of Topeka.

Steen's photograph looking east shows businesses and houses on Jackson Street and Kansas Avenue, the city's main business street. Near 9th Avenue directly east, First Baptist Church is under construction. The red brick Santa Fe office building spans half of the 900 block on Jackson. This Santa Fe building was replaced in 1924.

RIGHT: Landon State Office Building as it appears today.

SOUTH

South of the Capitol was the city's trolley and bus station, along with retail and residential neighborhoods. Businesses were later removed to build the Curtis State Office Building to the southeast and the Kansas Judicial Center.

To the south of the Capitol is 10th Avenue, bordered by Jackson Street on the east, at left; Van Buren, which is not pictured, would have been located to the south; and Harrison Street on the west, at right. Industrial buildings were located to the southeast with mostly residential area directly south.

RIGHT: View south of the Capitol showing the Kansas Judicial Center as it appears today.

WEST

Harrison Street to the west was once a residential neighborhood where some of the city's leaders lived. Many of the homes were removed when construction began on a state office building in 1954. The building opened in 1957 and in 1987 was dedicated the Docking State Office Building, for the 38th Governor of Kansas, Robert Docking. North of the office building are the Hiram Price Dillon House, built in 1914, and First Presbyterian Church, designed by statehouse architect George Ropes, built originally in 1884.

Along 9th Avenue, Wolf Hall at the College of the Sisters of Bethany can be seen at top. Toward 8th Avenue are First Presbyterian Church, and the city high school. Established on the northwest and southwest corners in 1871, Topeka High School was moved west to a new building near 10th Avenue and Polk Street in 1931.

RIGHT: View west of the Capitol as it appears today showing Docking State Office Building, the Dillon House, and First Presbyterian Church.

RIGHT: Memorial Hall, to the east of the Capitol along Jackson Street, as it appeared in 1914. Members of the public watched as Civil War veterans participated in the transfer of battle flags to the Kansas Historical Society's new location. Today Memorial Hall houses the offices of the Kansas Secretary of State and the Kansas Attorney General.

BELOW: The Curtis State Office Building, named for Kansan Charles Curtis, the only American Indian to serve as vice president of the United States. The building, located at the southeast corner of 10th Avenue and Jackson Street, opened in 2001 to house several state agencies.

OPPOSITE: Assumption Catholic Church and school, to the north of the Capitol along 8th Avenue, as it appeared in 1886. Established in 1862, this structure was built in 1882. A third structure, the current Mater Dei Catholic Church, was built in 1924.

TOP: The Hiram P. Dillon House, to the west of the Capitol along Harrison Street, as it appeared in the 1940s. Built in 1913, the house was designed in the Italian Renaissance style.

ABOVE: The Masonic Temple, to the south of the Capitol along 10th Avenue and Van Buren, as it appeared in the 1930s.

TOP: The Kansas Judicial Center, to the south of the Capitol, opened in 1978, and houses the Kansas Supreme Court and the Kansas Court of Appeals.

ABOVE: Docking State Office Building, to the west of the Capitol, pictured circa 1975 when a Standard Oil service station was located at 10th and Topeka Boulevard.

DOWNTOWN TOPEKA

Topeka quickly grew after its founding in December 1854. By the end of the year there were 130 new settlers in the community. The first stone building was located near 5th on Kansas Avenue and was used for the Topeka Constitutional Convention in fall 1855. When construction began on the Capitol in 1866, Topeka businesses along the dirt covered Kansas Avenue included groceries, banks, and dry goods. The city continued to grow along Kansas Avenue, spreading to the west along Jackson and Van Buren streets, and to the north of the Kansas River.

RIGHT: The west side of the 600 block of Quincy Street, one block east of Kansas Avenue, circa 1900.

BELOW: The east side of the 600 block of Kansas Avenue, 1930s.

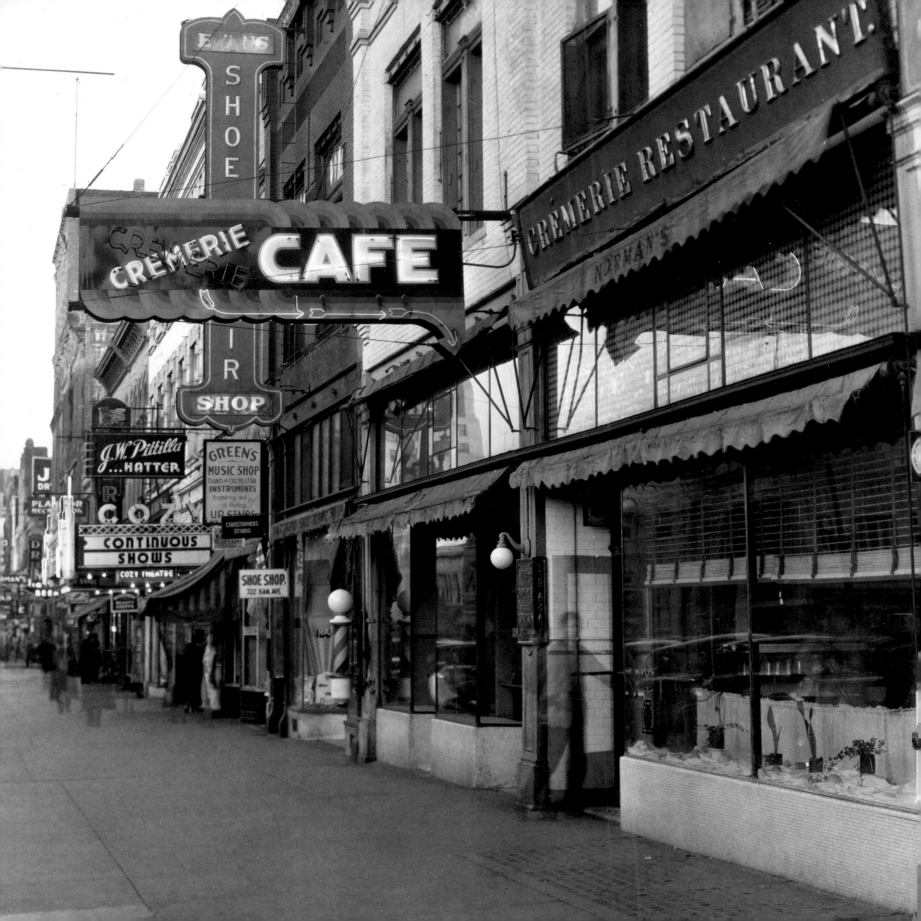